Music Reading *for Bass*

The Complete Guide

by Wendi Hrehovcsik

ISBN 978-0-7935-8197-9

7777 W. BLUEMOUND RD. P.O. BOX 13819 MILWAUKEE, WI 53213

Visit Hal Leonard Online at
www.halleonard.com

Table of Contents

Introduction

Music is a language, and the thrill of conversing and expressing ourselves within this language is generally what compels us to choose music as a hobby or profession. Learning to read music is therefore a natural step toward expanding our musical experience and fulfillment, as well as an essential goal for any competent, well-rounded musician.

This book takes at least three approaches to learning to read music on the bass:

- by string
- by key
- by position and scale form

In addition, this book includes an extensive exploration of rhythms, coverage of more advanced bass techniques like slides and ghost tones, and practical information on how to follow a chart, how to read from chord symbols, and how to create walking bass lines.

I sincerely hope the tools presented in this book provide you with the keys to unlocking your potential and lead you to many exciting musical encounters, both on the written page and off.

About the Author

Wendi Hrehovcsik has been an instructor at BIT since 1987. She currently plays and records in the Los Angeles area.

Chapter One

1

The Staff

The fundamentals of music are *pitch* and *rhythm,* which are organized in the form of notes and rests placed on a grid of five lines and four spaces. This grid is called a *staff.* The lines and spaces of the staff may be referred to numerically from the bottom up, so the bottom line would be the first line, etc.

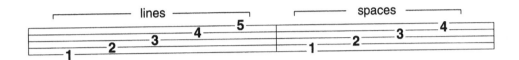

The names of the notes correspond to the first seven letters of the alphabet: A, B, C, D, E, F, and G. After G, the order repeats itself. In the bass clef, in which most music for the electric bass is written, the names of the lines, starting with the first line, are G, B, D, F, and A. The names of the spaces, starting with the first space, are A, C, E, and G.

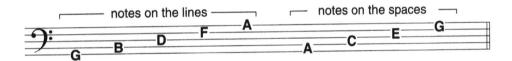

The Bass Clef

Music for the electric bass is usually written in *bass clef.* This symbol is derived from the old German way of writing "F." The two dots to the right of the bass clef symbol outline the note F on the staff. This is why the bass clef is also called the *F clef.*

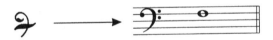

Notes

The length, or *duration,* of a note is determined by the type of note used and its relation to the meter of the music. Notes can contain three parts: a *head,* a *stem,* and a *flag.*

These are the most common note values for bass music:

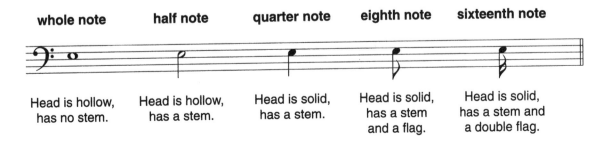

The *stem direction* of a note is determined by its placement on the staff, and sometimes by its relationship to the notes around it (if the stems are tied). Generally speaking, if the notehead lies on or below the second space, the stem direction is up. If the notehead lies on the third line or above, the stem direction is down.

Pitch

The highness or lowness of note, its *pitch,* is determined by the note's placement on the staff. The four open strings of the bass correspond to the *sound* of the following notes on the piano:

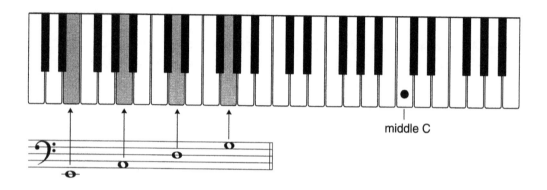

middle C

Notes for the bass are written an octave above where they sound on the piano. In other words, if a bassist plays the bass clef of a piano chart, the notes will sound one octave below what is actually written.

Intervals

The smallest distance, or *interval,* between two notes in Western music is called a *half step.* If you play any note on the bass and then play another note one fret higher, you have just played a half step. If you move two frets higher (two half steps up), you have moved up one *whole step.* If you play a note on one string and then slide up twelve frets on the same string and play the note there, you have played an *octave.*

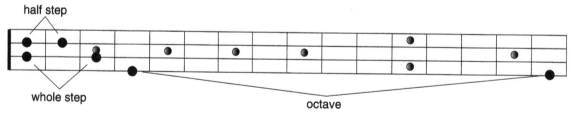

Accidentals

Any note can be raised or lowered a half step by placing an accidental directly before it.

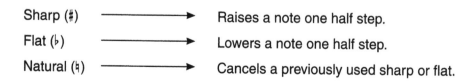

Sharp (♯) ──────────▶ Raises a note one half step.

Flat (♭) ──────────▶ Lowers a note one half step.

Natural (♮) ──────────▶ Cancels a previously used sharp or flat.

Ledger Lines

Notes higher or lower than the range of the staff must be written using *ledger lines.* Ledger lines should have the same spacing as the lines on the staff.

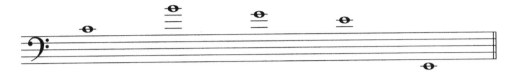

Bass Fretboard Diagrams

The following fretboard diagrams are included for your reference. Examine them now, and refer to them later if you need to check notes or positions later on in the book.

Chapter Two

Measures and Bar Lines

Music is divided into equal sections called *measures.* Measures are also referred to as bars. Measures are divided from each other by *bar lines.*

Time Signatures

The beat or pulse of a piece of music is shown by the *time signature,* which is located at the beginning of the music, after the clef sign. In a time signature, the top number indicates the number of beats per measure, while the bottom number indicates the type of note that receives one beat.

4 ← number of beats per measure
4 ← type of note that receives one beat

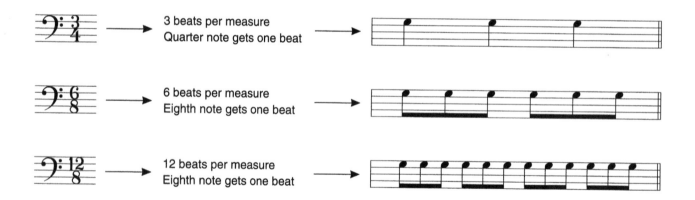

The most common time signature in music, from classical to heavy metal, is 4/4 time. Because of its common use, it is also referred to as *common time,* and can be written either as 4/4 or as C.

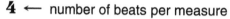 or

In 4/4, or common time, there are four beats per measure, and the quarter note receives the beat, so each measure must contain the equivalent of four quarter notes.

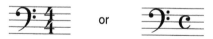

Counting Time

In common time, it is recommended you tap your foot on each quarter note while counting the division of beats out loud or silently in your head.

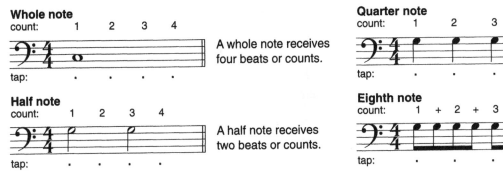

Whole note
A whole note receives four beats or counts.

Half note
A half note receives two beats or counts.

Quarter note
A quarter note receives one beat or counts.

Eighth note
(say: "one and two and…")
An eighth note receives one-half beat.

EXERCISE

Practice clapping the rhythms below. With each example, try to keep your foot tapping consistently on the quarter note. Count out loud the divisions: "1, 2, 3, 4," etc. Keep the tempo slow and steady.

Rests

A period of silence in music is indicated by a *rest.* For each note value, there is a comparable rest value. The counting of time remains constant whether counting notes or rests.

EXERCISE 1

EXERCISE 2

When working with eighth-note subdivisions, count "1+2+3+4+," etc.

Dotted Notes

A *dot* following a note or rest indicates this note or rest will receive the value of itself plus half again its own value. For example:

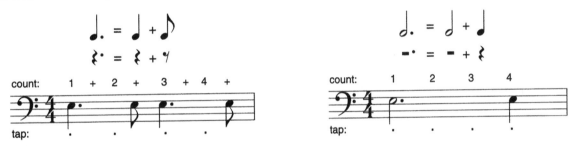

EXERCISE

Clap out these dotted-note rhythms. Remember to count out loud and keep your foot tapping the quarter note.

Chapter Three

3

Notes on the E String, Frets 1–5

Play these notes on the E string. Learn to recognize the notes both on the staff and on the fretboard. Notice that the notes on frets 2 and 4 each have two different note names. Two notes sounding the same but written differently are called *enharmonic equivalents*.

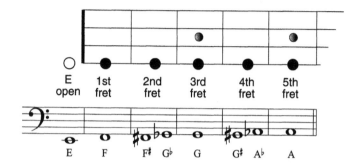

Play these exercises on the E string. Remember to count out loud and tap your foot, slowly and steadily. For the first few staves, fingerings are given as follows: 1=index, 2=middle, 3=ring, 4=pinkie. An arrow (→) indicates a shift in hand position.

EXERCISE 1

EXERCISE 2

EXERCISE 3: Bass Lines on the E String

Rules for Accidentals

- Sharps or flats denoted by the key signature do not need an accidental marking.

- If a note has been altered by a sharp or flat, it retains that alteration for the measure, unless canceled by a natural sign (♮). If necessary, it is also common practice to cancel the accidental in the measure immediately following, to avoid confusion.

Notes on the A String, Frets 1–5

Play these notes on the A string. Learn to recognize them on the staff and on the fretboard.

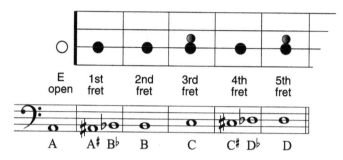

EXERCISE 1

EXERCISE 2

EXERCISE 3

EXERCISE 4

EXERCISE 5: Bass Lines on the A String

By now, you should be able to count and subdivide silently to yourself.

Notes on E and A Strings

EXERCISE 1: Bass Lines on the E and A Strings

Blues

Rock

Reggae

Bossa Nova

EXERCISE 2: Random Notes on the E and A Strings

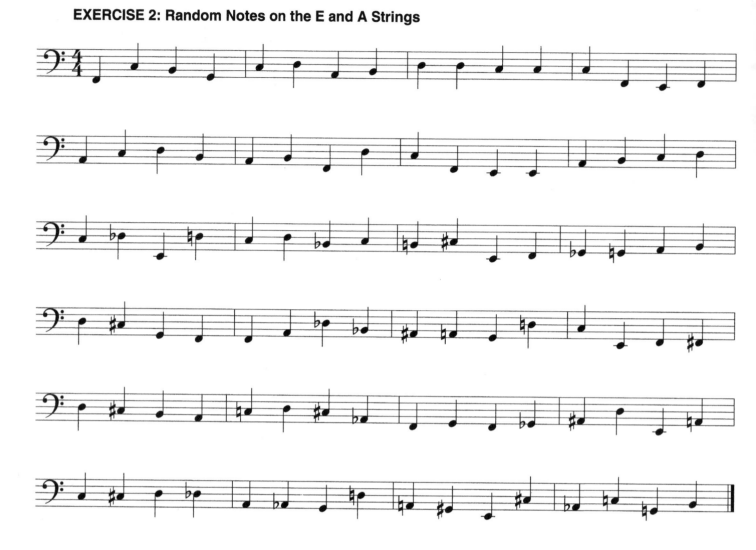

EXERCISE 3: Duet

Here is a duet to play with another bassist. The top part contains notes from the A string, and the bottom part contains notes from the E string.

Chapter Four

4

Notes on the D String, Frets 1–5

Play these notes on the D string. Learn to recognize them on the staff and on the fretboard. Try to read the notes and play them without looking at your bass.

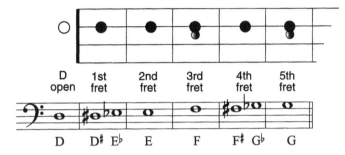

Play the following exercises on the D string, slowly and steadily. If you need to, mark in the counting divisions on top of the staff and the tap markings below, as shown in previous examples.

EXERCISE 1

EXERCISE 2

EXERCISE 3: More Reading on the D String

EXERCISE 4: Random Notes on the D String

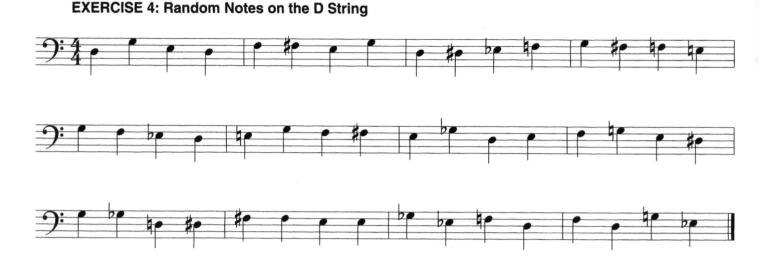

EXERCISE 5: Bass Lines on the D String

Play these at a slow tempo at first, then experiment with different tempos and feels.

Notes on the G String, Frets 1–5

Learn to play and recognize these notes on the G string. Try to look at the staff, not the bass.

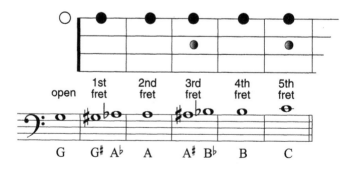

Play the following exercises on the G string, slowly and steadily. Write in counting divisions or fingerings only if you need to. Keep your foot tapping on the quarter-note pulse.

EXERCISE 1

EXERCISE 2: Random Notes on the G String

EXERCISE 3: Bass Lines on the G String

Notes on D and G Strings

EXERCISE: Reading on the D and G Strings

EXERCISE 2: Random Notes on D and G Strings

EXERCISE 3: Duet

Here is a duet to play with another bassist. The top part consists of notes from the G string, and the bottom part consists of notes from the D string. Play once through with one part, and then switch parts. Remember to count and to keep the time steady.

Chapter Five

5

More Eighth-Note Rhythms

Clap through these exercises, or play them on your bass.

EXERCISE 1

EXERCISE 2: Introducing the ♪♩ ♪ Rhythm

EXERCISE 3: With Dotted Quarter and Half Notes

Interval Studies

Play through these exercises entirely in the first position, keeping your first finger on the first fret, your second finger on the second fret, etc. Refer to the indicated fingerings if necessary.

EXERCISE 1: Fourths, Position I

EXERCISE 2: Fifths, Position I

Notes on All Four Strings

EXERCISE 1: Random Notes on E, A, D, and G Strings

EXERCISE 2: Bass Lines

Play these two bass lines using the notes from all four strings. Try to repeat each line three times without stopping or making a mistake.

EXERCISE 3: Duet

STUDY

Fill in notes to complete the measures below. Each measure must add up to the equivalent of four quarter notes. Use only the E note as written.

Now recopy the rhythms, but use a variety of notes from those we have covered so far. Play what you have written.

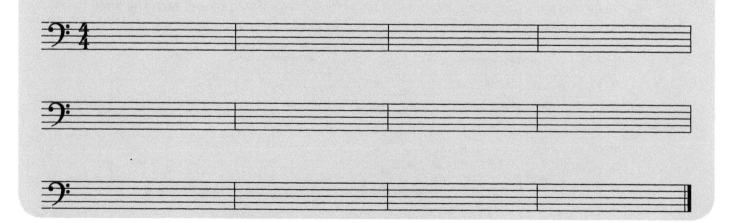

Chapter Six

6

Sixteenth-Note Rhythms

In this chapter, we will work with sixteenth notes and sixteenth rests. One measure of 4/4 time is equal to 16 sixteenth notes. These are counted as follows:

Notice you should still be tapping your foot on *each quarter note.* Also, the "and" of the beat remains at the midway point between beats.

Sixteenth notes may be connected in groups of four within the same beat, or in combination with an eighth note.

Beamed sixteenth notes should only occur within the same beat; they should never be beamed over the beat or over the bar. Note the following examples.

Incorrect   Correct

A sixteenth rest is similar to an eighth rest but has two flags on the stem. When combined with rests, sixteenth notes may or may not be tied together with a beam.

Practice these sixteenth-note and eighth-note rhythms. Repeat each bar several times before going on to the next. Remember to tap your foot on the quarter note, slowly and steadily.

Exercise 1

Exercise 2

Exercise 3

Exercise 4

Exercise 5

Exercise 6: Sixteenth-Note Rhythms with Pitches Added

Chapter Seven

7

Reading within a Key

The *key signature* is found at the beginning of the staff between the clef and the time signature. Occasionally, a piece of music may move through more than one key and therefore contain two or more different key signatures, but more often the same key signature is retained throughout an entire piece.

A sharp or flat in the key signature means that every note of that name is altered as such unless preceded by another accidental.

Major keys are based on major scales and contain the same sharps or flats as their namesake.

Key of C, no sharps or flats

(C major scale, no sharps or flats)

Key of F, one flat

(F major scale, one flat)

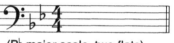

Key of B♭, two flats

(B♭ major scale, two flats)

Reading in the Key of C Major

Begin by playing a one-octave C major scale. Below is a diagram for a C major scale using the notes studied so far. The root of the scale is circled, as is the octave.

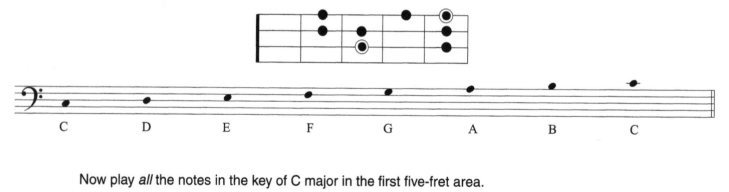

C   D   E   F   G   A   B   C

Now play *all* the notes in the key of C major in the first five-fret area.

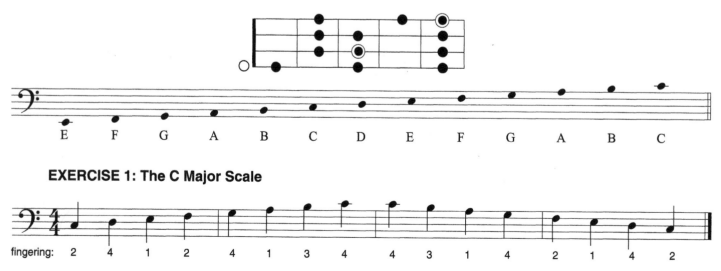

E   F   G   A   B   C   D   E   F   G   A   B   C

EXERCISE 1: The C Major Scale

fingering: 2   4   1   2   4   1   3   4   4   3   1   4   2   1   4   2

EXERCISE 2: Thirds in C

EXERCISE 3: Melody in C

EXERCISE 4: Bass Lines, Key of C

Reading in the Key of F Major

Notes in the key of F major, first five-fret area, roots circled:

E F G A B♭ C D E F G A B♭ C

EXERCISE 1: The F Major Scale

Try managing these shifts by stretching your left hand and pivoting your thumb.

fingering: 1 → 2   4 → 1   2   4   1   2   2   1   4   2 → 1 → 4   2 → 1

EXERCISE 2: Melody in F

EXERCISE 3: Thirds in F

EXERCISE 4: Bass Lines, Key of F

1

2

Reading in the Key of B♭ Major

Notes in the key of B♭ major, first five-fret area, roots circled:

F G A B♭ C D E♭ F G A B♭ C

EXERCISE 1: The B♭ Major Scale

fingering: 1 → 2   4 → 1 → 2   4   1   2   2   1   4   2 → 1 → 4   2 → 1

EXERCISE 2: Fourths in B♭

EXERCISE 3: Etude in B♭ Major

EXERCISE 4: Bass Lines, Key of B♭

①

②

The Sixteenth-Note Challenge

Play this sixteenth-note exercise slowly, one measure at a time. Then try to pick up the tempo and repeat it three times without a mistake.

EXERCISE

Chapter Eight

8

Reading in the Key of G Major

Notes in the key of G major, first five-fret area, roots circled:

E   F♯   G   A   B   C   D   E   F♯   G   A   B   C

EXERCISE 1: The G Major Scale

fingering: 2   4   1   2   4   1   3   4   4   3   1   4   2   1   4   2

EXERCISE 2: Fourths in G

EXERCISE 3: Etude in G

EXERCISE 4: Bass Lines, Key of G

Rock

Latin Funk

Rock

EXERCISES: Duet in G

Fine

D.C. al Fine

Reading in the Key of D with Extended Fingerings

Notes in the key of D major, first five-fret area and extending to the high D on the G string:

EXERCISE 1: The D Major Scale

EXERCISE 2: Walking Bass Line—Blues in D

EXERCISE 3: Bass Line, Key of D

EXERCISE 4: Etude in D

Mark in the shifting for the extended fingerings.

More Sixteenth-Note Rhythms

Clap this exercise slowly. Keep your foot tapping on the quarter notes and a metronome on the sixteenth-note subdivision.

EXERCISE 5

Chapter Nine

9

In reading music, one must constantly negotiate shifting from one part of the fretboard to another in order to reach the higher or lower notes. In order to facilitate this navigation of the fretboard and to demonstrate it in the following chapters, the location of the left hand on the fretboard will be defined in two ways: *position* and *scale form.*

Position

Position refers to what fret the first finger of the left hand rests on, with the other three fingers following in a one-finger-per-fret manner. For example, the first finger on the first fret would be Position 1, the first finger on the fourth fret would be Position 4, and so on.

Scale Forms

Scale form refers to any of the five scale forms derived from the major scale. These are named according to the step of the major scale they begin with and are diagrammed below. Try to memorize them as quickly as possible and practice them in all keys; they can be tremendously helpful in navigating the fretboard.

Because there are seven steps in a major scale, there could actually be seven possible scale forms. However, the two points in the major scale at which half steps occur (between steps 3 and 4 and between steps 7 and 8) eliminate the need for separate forms at these two positions. Thus, scale forms 3 and 4 become Scale Form 3-4, and scale form 7 is effectively contained in Scale Form 1. This leaves us with just the five forms.

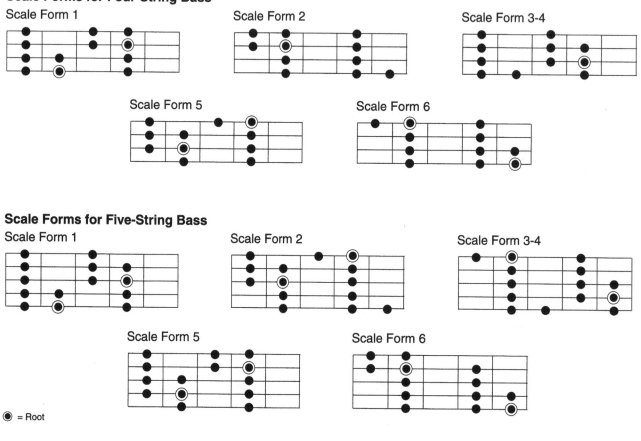

Scale Forms for Four-String Bass

Scale Form 1   Scale Form 2   Scale Form 3-4

Scale Form 5   Scale Form 6

Scale Forms for Five-String Bass

Scale Form 1   Scale Form 2   Scale Form 3-4

Scale Form 5   Scale Form 6

◉ = Root

Scale Forms for Six-String Bass

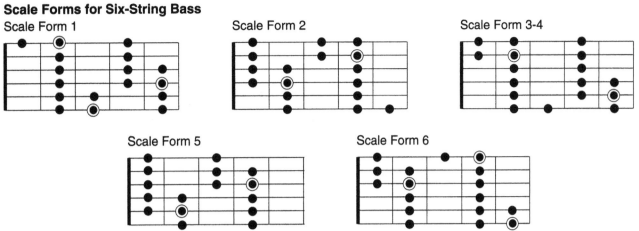

Scale Form 1   Scale Form 2   Scale Form 3-4

Scale Form 5   Scale Form 6

◉ = Root

Exercise: All Scale Forms, Key of G Major

Play this exercise in the key of G, using the fingerings written underneath. Watch for the shift cues, which indicate a change of hand position.

Chapter Ten

Key of E, Second Position, Scale Form 2

This scale form is slightly expanded to include the open E string.

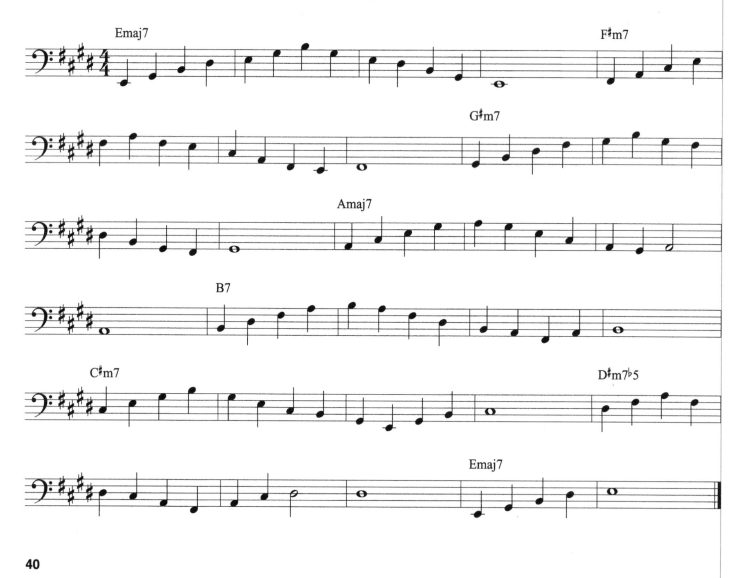

EXERCISE: Diatonic Arpeggios, Key of E, Scale Form 2

Because bass players are usually outlining chords, it is important to know where the diatonic arpeggios are located in every position on the fretboard. Keep your fingers planted firmly in Scale Form 2 here, and listen for the harmony as you play through this exercise.

Key of E, Fourth Position, Scale Form 3-4

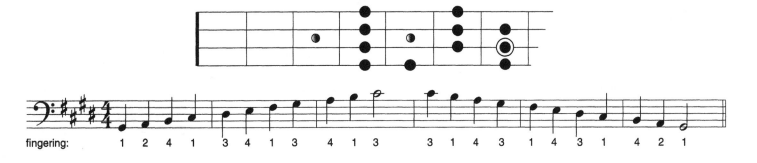

fingering: 1 2 4 1 3 4 1 3 4 1 3 3 1 4 3 1 4 3 1 4 2 1

EXERCISE: Study in Diatonic Arpeggios, Key of E, Scale Form 3-4

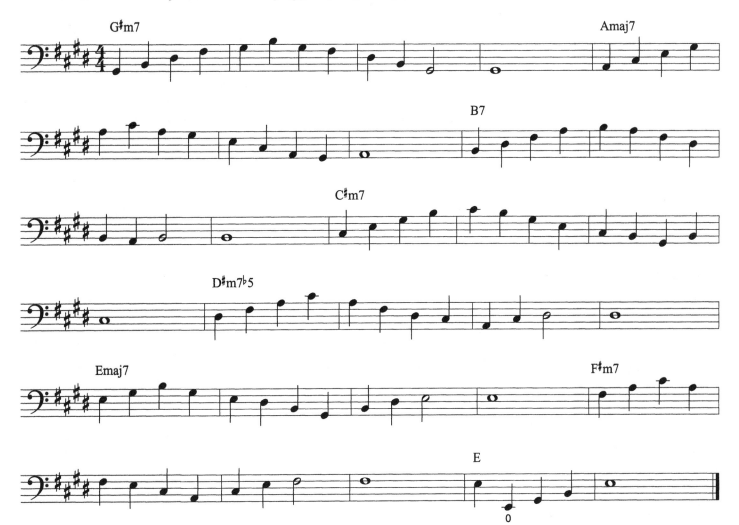

Combining Scale Forms 2 and 3-4

EXERCISE 1

Play the following piece using the scale forms suggested in the boxes. The open E-string pedal can be played in either form.

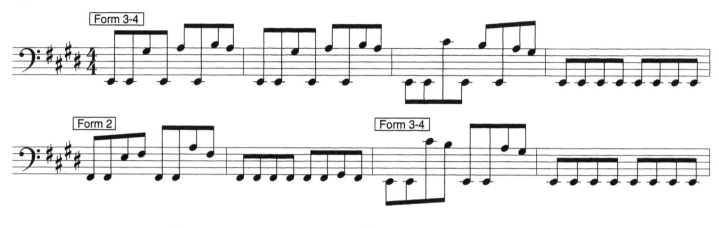

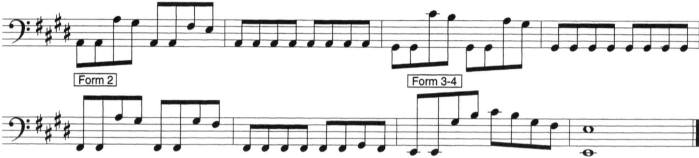

EXERCISE 2: Duet

Play this duet using Scale Form 3-4 for the top part and Scale Form 2 for the bottom part. Remember to keep your hands in the scale form position, with fingers close to the fretboard.

Chapter Eleven

11

Key of E♭, Fifth Position, Scale Form 5

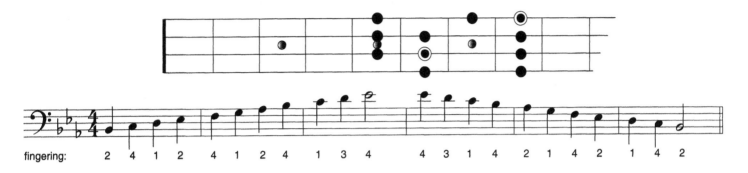

EXERCISE: Study in Diatonic Arpeggios, Key of E♭, Scale Form 5

Play this exercise using the fingerings given. All notes are within Scale Form 5

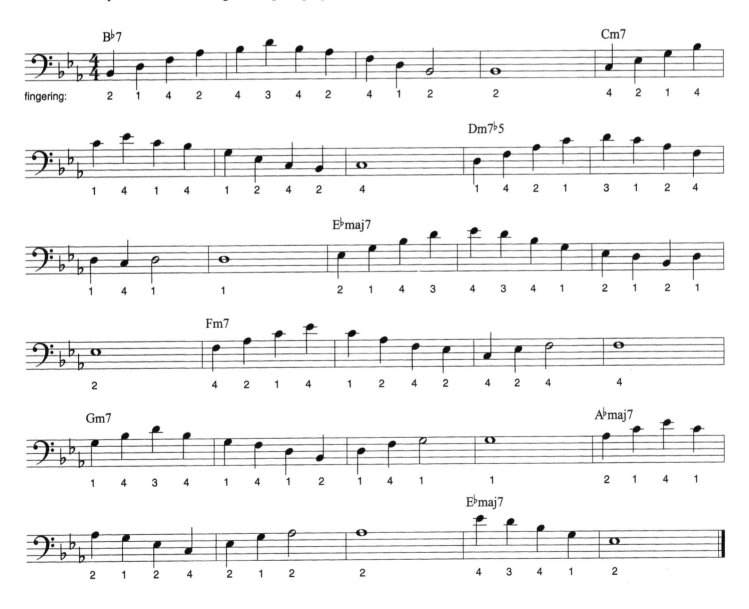

Key of E♭, Eighth Position, Scale Form 6

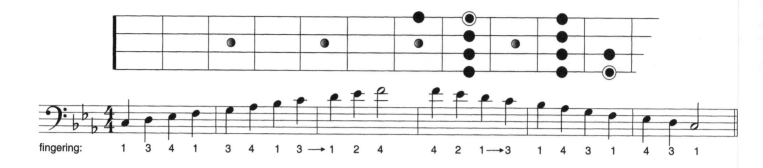

EXERCISE: Study in Diatonic Arpeggios, Key of E♭, Scale Form 6

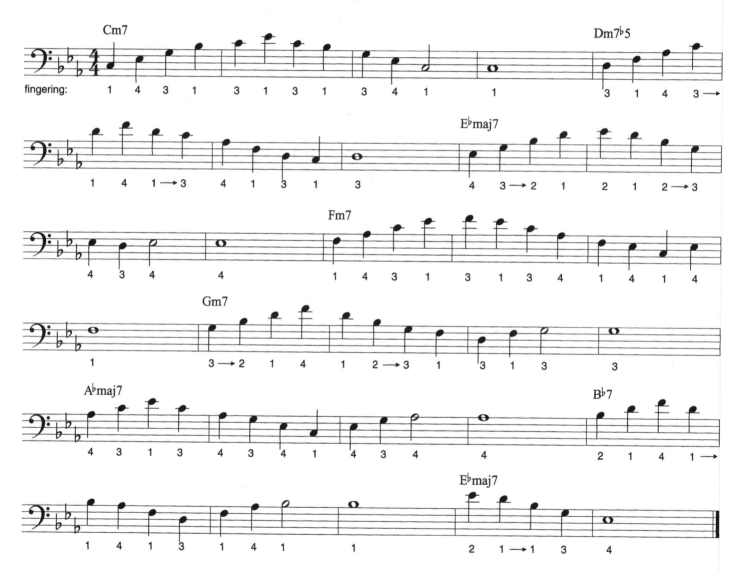

Combining Scale Forms 5 and 6

EXERCISE 1: Etude in E♭

Start this exercise in Scale Form 5, then make the shift to Scale Form 6 in measure 8, using the fingerings indicated. Then play it again, shifting in a different spot.

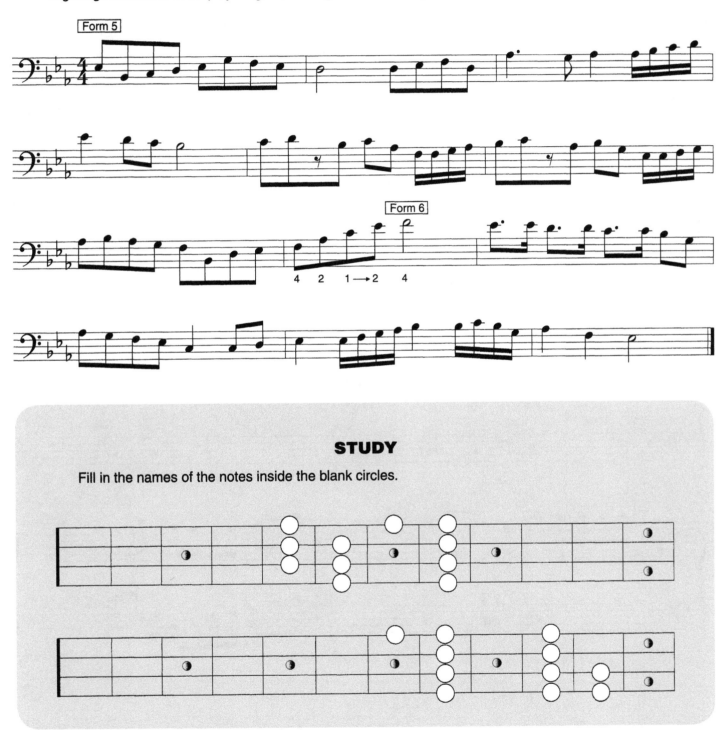

STUDY

Fill in the names of the notes inside the blank circles.

EXERCISE 2: Duet in C Minor

This reggae duet can be played with either straight eighths or swing eighths. The top part can be played entirely in Scale Form 6 (Key of E♭). The lower part requires shifting. Find a logical shifting point, and mark it with shifting arrows in the score.

Chapter Twelve

12

Eighth-Note Triplets

Triplets are a group of three notes that occupy the time equivalent of two of the same kind of note. For example, two eighth notes are normally equal to one quarter note, or one beat in 4/4 time. So, an eighth-note triplet (indicated by the number "3" placed above or below the three-note grouping) is also equal to one quarter note when counting time.

Quarter Notes

Eighth Notes

Eighth-Note Triplets

To practice feeling the rhythm of the eighth-note triplet, begin by tapping your foot steadily on the quarter-note pulse and saying the three-syllable word "blueberry" on each tap. If you are stretching the word evenly between each beat, each syllable will fall on an eighth note.

Next, try replacing the word "blueberry" with the more traditional counting, using the word "triplet" divided into three syllables.

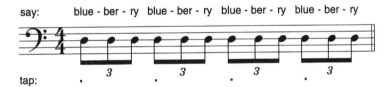

EXERCISE 1

Practice clapping these eighth-note triplet rhythms. Note the alternate method of counting, using "1-trip-let, 2-trip-let," etc. This allows you to better keep track of which beat you are on.

EXERCISE 3: Rests within the Triplet

Clap these rhythms, which focus on eighth rests within the triplet figure.

EXERCISE 4: Combining Eighth Notes with Eighth-Note Triplets

EXERCISE 5: Eighth-Note Triplets with Sixteenth Notes and Rests

EXERCISE 6: Three Bass Lines Containing Eighth-Note Triplets

STUDY

Fill in the missing beats with eighth-note triplets.

Using the rhythms above, add notes from the key of C major, second position, Scale Form 5. Now play your exercise.

Chapter Thirteen

13

Quarter-Note Triplets

As stated in the previous chapter, triplets are a group of three notes equivalent in time to two notes of the same type. A quarter-note triplet is three quarter notes which take up the same time as two quarter notes.

Half notes

Quarter notes

Quarter-note triplets

One quarter note of a quarter-note triplet is equal to two eighth notes of an eighth-note triplet. In counting quarter-note triplets, one must first think in eighth-note triplet division, then give value to *every other* note. Tapping of the foot should remain, as always, on the quarter notes.

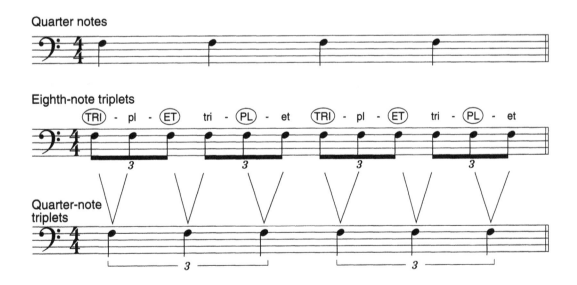

EXERCISE1 : Quarter-Note Triplets Combined with Eighth-Note Triplets and Quarter Notes

Clap the following rhythms, keeping your foot tapping on quarter notes and maintaining an eighth-note triplet division of the beat. Repeat each measure at least twice before moving on to the next.

EXERCISE 2: Quarter-Note Triplets Combined with Eighth Notes

Clap these rhythms, keeping your foot tapping on the quarter note. In these exercises, you must switch back and forth between triplet and straight eighth-note division, so try to look ahead in the measure and be ready for the division needed.

EXERCISE 3: Adding Sixteenth Notes to Quarter-Note Triplet Rhythms

EXERCISE 4: Rests within the Quarter-Note Triplet

EXERCISE 5: Bass Lines with Quarter-Note Triplets

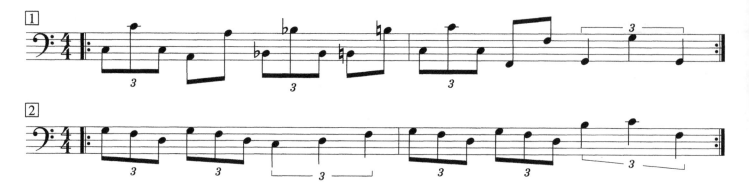

EXERCISE 6: Duet

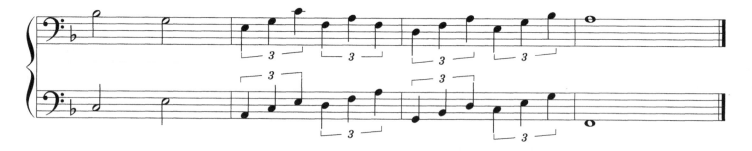

Chapter Fourteen

14

Ties

A *tie* is a curved line that connects two or more consecutive notes of the same pitch. When notes are tied, the first note is struck then held through the duration of the notes joined by the tie.

EXERCISE 1

Clap these rhythms, then play them, holding the notes for their full value.

EXERCISE 2

Play these two lines with ties.

EXERCISE 3: Same Line, Different Ties

Play the first bass line below several times until it becomes very comfortable to execute, then try the following three variations of the same line with the ties added. Notice how the same line takes on an entirely different feel when ties are added in different places.

Variation 1

Variation 2

Variation 3

Accent Markings

Accent markings are used to place emphasis on particular notes. There are different types of accent markings for different types of emphasis. These are some of the most common:

(·)   Staccato—play the note very short.

(∧)   Play the note with a sharp attack, short and percussive. More intensity than (·).

(>)   Less percussive and longer in value than (∧).

(–)   Note is held for its full value.

(≥)   Note is stressed and held for its full value.

Accents are most commonly written above the note but can also be written below the note when the stem direction is upward.

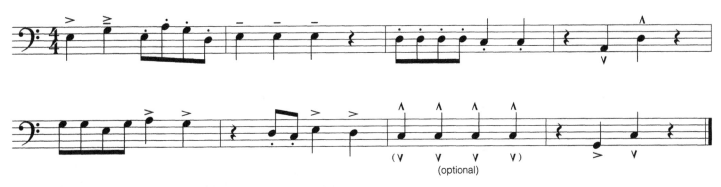

Dynamic Markings

Dynamic markings indicate degrees of loudness. They are located beneath the staff, slightly before the note or notes affected. These are some of the most common:

(***pp***) pianissimo: very soft   (***p***)   piano: soft

(***mp***) mezzo piano: moderately soft   (***mf***) mezzo forte: medium loud

(***f***)   forte: loud   (***ff***) fortissimo: very loud

(***sf***)   sforzando: with a sudden strong accent   (***fp***) forte piano: loud followed by soft

(⟨) *cresc.,* crescendo: increasing loudness

(⟩) *decresc.* or *dim.,* decrescendo or diminuendo: decreasing loudness

Play the following exercise, paying attention to the dynamic markings.

Slides

A slide is indicated by a straight line connecting two notes, or a line by itself preceding a note.

For a slide between two notes, sound the first note, then slide up to the second, sounding the second note but not striking it. For a slide preceding a particular note, sound the string as you slide up to the desired note.

Practice these slides:

Ghost Notes

Ghost notes are a percussive technique created by dampening or deadening the string with the left hand while striking or pressing the string with the right, not quite hard enough for a note to sound. They are notated using an "x" instead of a notehead.

Try this bass line using ghost notes:

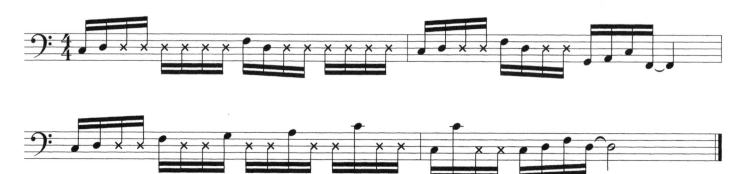

Chapter Fifteen

15

Following the "Road Map" of a Chart

There can be many directions to follow in reading a chart. Here is a short glossary of some of the most common terms and their symbols. Use it to read your way through the following chart.

Intro   An introductory passage or groove preceding the main body of a tune.

Vamp   A passage repeated over and over, either a set number of times or until a cue is given to move on.

On Cue   Marks a section of the music that begins when a signal is given by the conductor or band leader.

Repeat   Signs (‖: :‖) at the beginning and ending of a section which indicate the repetition of that section. Sometimes separate endings are required, and are marked with ending signs such as ⌐1.   and ⌐2.

D.C.   *Da Capo,* indicates that a piece of music is to be repeated from the beginning.

D.S.   *Dal Segno,* indicates that a piece of music is to be repeated not from the beginning, but from a specific place marked by the sign (𝄋).

Coda (⊕)   Concluding section or passage. *Al Coda* = to the coda.

8va   Indicates that a section is to be played up an octave. The affected section will also be marked with a broken line above the staff.

Fine   To close or end.

EXERCISE 1: Tune

EXERCISE 2: Duet

Try working out this short but challenging duet with a partner.

STUDY

Compose your own bass line or melody, using the following directives: on cue, repeats, D.S. al Coda, and 8va. Use a variety of rhythms.

Chapter Sixteen

16

Reading from Chord Symbols

Bass players are frequently required to read from chord symbols. Because this can be a large percentage of the type of reading encountered, it brings to light other skills necessary outside of basic note-and-rhythm proficiency. To be adept at reading from chord symbols, one must:

- Have extensive knowledge of chord structure and harmony.

- Be familiar with how the bass functions in a variety of styles of music.

- Understand the role of the bass player—which normally consists of either outlining the sound of a chord while laying down a good, solid groove, or creating a bass line supportive to the melody and integral to the rest of the band.

Completing a Bass Line

Sometimes, a sample bass line is given to establish the basic groove, and you are expected to continue the same line, altering it to fit over different chords. For example:

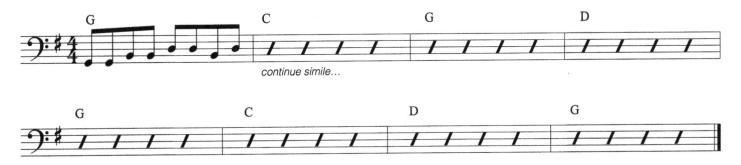

First, analyze the bass line. Our example contains the root, 3rd, and 5th of the chord.

Then, create a similar line over the rest of the chord changes. You should come up with the following bass line for our example, if you use the same pattern throughout:

The bass line above consists of all major triads; therefore, the line can be played using the same fingering pattern and simply shifting to a new root position for each chord change. However, most progressions contain varying qualities of chords, so the same fingering would not work throughout, even though the sequence of notes in relation to each chord remains consistent. This makes it important to know theory and chord structure instead of relying solely on the fingering pattern. Analyze the following bass line, then play a similar pattern over the other chords. Make necessary alterations in the fingering pattern to fit the chord (5 to ♭5, ♭7 to maj7, etc.).

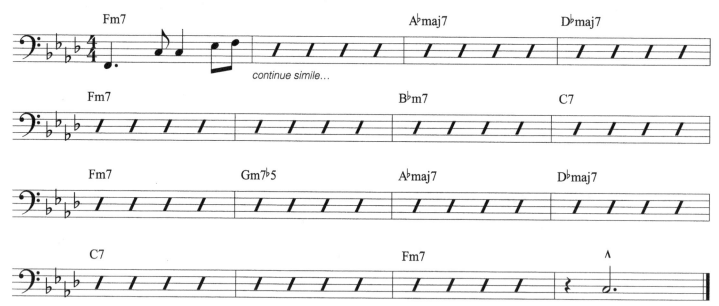

This bass line is a two-bar phrase containing non-chord tones, or notes not found within the chord. Analyze it, and then play it through the other changes.

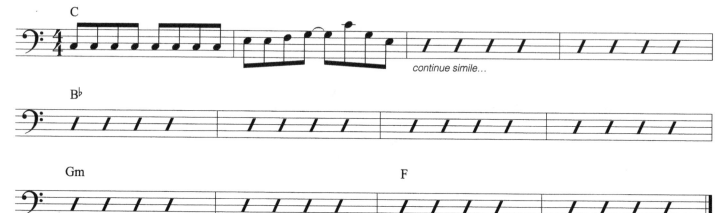

Here's one more, this time with a shuffle feel.

Walking Bass Lines

Another common thing to see in music written for bass is the instruction to "create a walking bass line" over a set of changes. To "walk" a bass line simply means to outline the sound of each chord in quarter notes. There are many techniques for creating a walking bass line, but a good place to start is to arpeggiate the chord for the first three beats (usually starting with the root on beat 1) then fill in beat 4 with a guide tone leading into the next measure. A *guide tone* (GT) is a note one half step above or below the targeted note. A guide tone on beat 4 may be leading to the root of the next chord, or if there is more than one measure of the same chord, to another chord tone within that chord. For example:

Here's another walking bass line using the same formula, this time over seventh chords.

STUDY

Analyze this sample bass line, and then continue the pattern over the remaining progression.

Now try this two-bar sample:

Using the chord tone/guide tone formula, create a walking bass line for the following progressions.

①   Em   Am   Dm   G7

C   Am   Dm   B7

②   E♭maj7   Am   Dm7♭5   G7♭9

Cm7   B♭m7   E♭7

A♭maj7   B♭7   E♭maj7   Cm7

F7   Fm7   B♭7